Valentine Kisses

2 egg whites
Pinch cream of tartar
½ cup sugar
Pink or red food coloring
Unsweetened cocoa powder (optional)

1. Preheat oven to 250°F. Line cookie sheets with parchment paper.

2. Beat egg whites in medium bowl with electric mixer at high speed until foamy. Add cream of tartar and beat until soft peaks form. Add sugar, 2 tablespoons at a time, beating until stiff and glossy. Stir in food coloring until batter is dark pink. (Color will lighten during baking, so batter should be darker than desired shade of pink.)

3. Drop meringue by tablespoonfuls, 1 inch apart, onto prepared cookie sheets. (Or pipe 1-inch mounds of meringue using pastry bag fitted with large writing tip.)

4. Bake about 30 minutes or until firm. Turn oven off; let cookies stand in oven 1 hour. Remove from oven; cool completely. Sprinkle lightly with cocoa, if desired.

Makes about 5 dozen cookies

Chocolate Chip Valentine Kisses: Prepare recipe as directed, gently folding in ¾ cup mini semisweet chocolate chips just before adding the food coloring.

Valentine Kisses

Cheesy Heart Breadsticks

  1 teaspoon Italian seasoning
¼ teaspoon red pepper flakes
  1 loaf (16 ounces) frozen white or wheat bread dough, thawed
  2 tablespoons olive oil
  1 cup (4 ounces) shredded Italian cheese blend

1. Preheat oven to 375°F. Line two baking sheets with parchment paper. Combine Italian seasoning and red pepper flakes in small bowl.

2. Divide dough into 8 equal pieces. Working with one piece at a time, roll dough between hands into 14-inch rope. Shape ropes into hearts on prepared baking sheets; pinch ends together to seal.

3. Brush hearts with oil; sprinkle evenly with Italian seasoning mixture. Sprinkle with cheese, pressing cheese in gently to adhere to dough.

4. Bake about 18 minutes or until golden brown and cheese is melted.

Makes 8 breadsticks

Tip Be sure to plan ahead and allow time for the dough to thaw. Frozen bread dough takes 2 to 3 hours to thaw at room temperature. Or, the dough may be placed in the refrigerator overnight; it will take 10 to 12 hours to thaw in the refrigerator.

Cheesy Heart Breadsticks

Raspberry Crispy Hearts

¼ cup (½ stick) butter
1 package (10½ ounces) mini marshmallows
⅛ teaspoon salt
½ cup seedless raspberry jam
Pink or red food coloring (optional)
6 cups crisp rice cereal
2 cups milk or semisweet chocolate chips, melted

1. Spray 13×9-inch baking pan with nonstick cooking spray. Melt butter in large saucepan over medium heat. Add marshmallows and salt; cook and stir until mixture is melted and smooth.

2. Stir in jam until well blended. Add food coloring, if desired, a few drops at a time, until desired shade of pink is reached. Stir in cereal until completely blended.

3. Immediately scoop mixture into prepared pan with spatula; spread into even layer with dampened hands. (Mixture will be very sticky.) Let stand about 1 hour or until completely cool, or refrigerate to speed up cooling.

4. Remove bars from pan to cutting board. Spray 3-inch heart-shaped cookie cutter with nonstick cooking spray; cut out hearts from bars.

5. Spread melted chocolate over each heart; use toothpick to create swirls in chocolate.

Makes about 2 dozen hearts

Note: These bars are best eaten the day they are made.

Raspberry Crispy Hearts

Cherry Berry Heart Tarts

  1 can (14½ ounces) red tart cherries in water
  ¾ cup plus 1 tablespoon sugar, divided
  2 tablespoons cornstarch
  ¼ teaspoon salt
  1 teaspoon lemon juice
  1 cup frozen raspberries (not in syrup), thawed and drained
  1 package (15 ounces) refrigerated pie crusts (2 crusts)
  2 tablespoons milk

1. Drain cherries, reserving liquid. Combine ¾ cup sugar, cornstarch and salt in medium saucepan. Stir in ⅓ cup cherry liquid and lemon juice until blended. Stir in cherries; bring to a simmer over medium heat. Cook and stir about 6 minutes or until thickened. Gently stir in raspberries; set aside to cool.

2. Meanwhile, preheat oven to 400°F. Line small cookie sheet with parchment paper. Unfold pie crusts on work surface; cut out 20 circles with 3-inch round cookie cutter. Cut out 20 hearts from dough scraps with ½-inch heart-shaped cookie cutter.*

3. Place heart cutouts on prepared cookie sheet. Brush with milk; sprinkle with remaining 1 tablespoon sugar. Bake about 7 minutes or until golden brown. Remove to wire rack to cool.

4. Press dough circles into 20 ungreased mini (1¾-inch) muffin cups and flute edges. Spoon about 1 tablespoon fruit filling into each cup.

5. Bake 15 minutes or until crust is golden brown and filling is bubbly. Cool tarts in pans 5 minutes; remove to wire racks to cool completely. Place 1 heart cutout in center of each tart.   *Makes 20 tarts*

If you don't have a small heart-shaped cookie cutter, you can cut out the hearts with scissors.

Cherry Berry Heart Tarts

Pizza Love

20 slices pepperoni or turkey pepperoni
  Olive oil
 1 loaf (16 ounces) frozen white bread dough, thawed
 6 tablespoons marinara or pizza sauce
 1 cup (4 ounces) shredded Italian or pizza cheese blend
½ teaspoon dried oregano

1. Preheat oven to 400°F. Line large baking sheet with parchment paper. Cut pepperoni slices into heart shapes with scissors; set aside.

2. Coat work surface lightly with oil. Divide dough into 4 equal pieces; stretch and roll out each piece into 7-inch circle on oiled surface. Shape circle into heart shape by pinching dough into point at bottom of circle and pulling down top of circle (opposite point) to form top of heart. Place hearts on prepared baking sheet.

3. Bake 5 minutes. Remove from oven; press crust back into heart shape if some of shape was lost during baking.

4. Spread 1½ tablespoons marinara sauce over each crust, leaving 1-inch border. Sprinkle cheese over sauce; top with 5 pepperoni slices. Sprinkle with oregano.

5. Bake about 15 minutes or until crust is golden brown and cheese is melted.

Makes 4 individual pizzas

Pizza Love

Black & White Heart Cookies

½ cup (1 stick) butter, softened
⅔ cup sugar
1 egg
1½ teaspoons vanilla
1½ cups flour
1 teaspoon CALUMET® Baking Powder
¼ teaspoon salt
1 package (8 squares) BAKER'S® Semi-Sweet Baking Chocolate, melted

BEAT butter and sugar in large bowl with electric mixer on medium speed until light and fluffy. Blend in egg and vanilla. Mix flour, baking powder and salt. Add to butter mixture; beat until well blended. Cover and refrigerate 1 hour.

ROLL out dough to ⅛-inch thickness on lightly floured surface. Cut out with 2-inch heart-shaped cookie cutter. Place, 2 inches apart, on parchment paper-covered baking sheet. Refrigerate 30 minutes.

PREHEAT oven to 350°F. Bake cookies 10 minutes or until edges are lightly browned. Cool. Dip 1 side of each cookie in chocolate. Place on wire racks; let stand until chocolate is firm.

Makes about 4 dozen cookies or 24 servings (2 cookies each)

Jazz it Up: Bake cookies and dip in chocolate as directed. Immediately sprinkle with red, white and/or pink sprinkles. Place on wire racks; let stand until chocolate is firm.

Prep Time: 20 minutes
Total Time: 2 hours (includes refrigerating)

Black & White Heart Cookies

Flourless Chocolate Cupcake Hearts

20 heart-shaped foil baking cups
 4 ounces bittersweet chocolate, finely chopped
½ cup (1 stick) butter, cubed
 2 tablespoons raspberry liqueur
¾ cup granulated sugar
 3 eggs, separated
½ cup unsweetened cocoa powder
   Dash salt
 1 package (12 ounces) frozen raspberries, thawed
¼ cup superfine or powdered sugar
   Fresh raspberries (optional)

1. Preheat oven to 350°F. Spray 10 baking cups with nonstick cooking spray. Place each sprayed cup into second unsprayed cup for stability. Arrange cups on rimmed baking sheet.

2. Heat chocolate and butter in medium saucepan over very low heat until melted, stirring frequently. Remove from heat. Stir in raspberry liqueur; set aside to cool slightly.

3. Beat granulated sugar and egg yolks in large bowl with electric mixer at medium speed until light and fluffy. Add chocolate mixture; beat until blended. Sift cocoa into mixture; stir by hand until blended.

4. Beat egg whites and salt in medium bowl with electric mixer at high speed until stiff peaks form. *Do not overbeat.* Gently fold beaten egg whites into chocolate mixture. Pour batter into prepared cups, filling half full.

5. Bake 10 to 12 minutes or until edges are set and centers are still slightly soft. Remove to wire rack to cool completely. Remove cupcakes from baking cups.

6. Place thawed raspberries in fine mesh strainer over bowl; mash with back of spoon to crush berries and remove seeds. Stir superfine sugar into strained raspberries. To serve, drizzle raspberry sauce on plate; top with cupcake. Garnish with fresh raspberries.

Makes 10 cupcakes

Flourless Chocolate Cupcake Heart

Sweetheart Sandwiches

8 slices rustic Italian bread
6 tablespoons chocolate hazelnut spread
4 tablespoons raspberry jam

1. Cut bread slices into hearts with 3- to 4-inch heart-shaped cookie cutter, knife or scissors.

2. Spread chocolate spread on 4 bread slices; spread jam on remaining 4 bread slices. Put bread slices together to form 4 sandwiches.

3. Spray large skillet with nonstick cooking spray; heat over medium heat. Add sandwiches to skillet; cook about 2 minutes per side or until lightly toasted and chocolate begins to melt.

Makes 4 sandwiches

Cherry Cheese Sweetheart Sandwiches: Omit chocolate spread and raspberry jam. Spread 4 bread slices with cherry jam; top each with 1 ounce white Cheddar cheese and remaining bread slice. Toast sandwiches in skillet as directed.

Tip To create broken heart sandwiches, cut a zig-zag line down the center of each sandwich with a small knife after cooking.

Sweetheart Sandwiches

Chocolate Lovers' Cupcakes

¾ cup all-purpose flour
½ cup unsweetened cocoa powder
1 teaspoon baking powder
½ teaspoon salt
½ cup (1 stick) butter, softened
1 cup plus 2 tablespoons granulated sugar
2 eggs
1 teaspoon vanilla
½ cup whole milk
1½ cups chocolate frosting
Powdered sugar

1. Preheat oven to 350°F. Line 12 standard (2½-inch) muffin cups with paper baking cups.

2. Combine flour, cocoa, baking powder and salt in small bowl. Beat butter in large bowl with electric mixer at medium speed until creamy. Add granulated sugar; beat 3 to 4 minutes. Add eggs, one at a time, beating well after each addition. Beat in vanilla. Add flour mixture alternately with milk, beginning and ending with flour mixture. Spoon batter into prepared muffin cups, filling two-thirds full.

3. Bake about 20 minutes or until toothpick inserted into centers comes out clean. Cool cupcakes in pan 10 minutes; remove to wire rack to cool completely.

4. Microwave frosting in medium microwavable bowl on MEDIUM (50%) 30 seconds; stir. Microwave at additional 15-second intervals until frosting is melted. (Consistency will be thin.) Dip tops of cupcakes in melted frosting; return to wire rack to allow frosting to set. (Frosting may need to be reheated several times to maintain melted consistency.)

5. When frosting is set, place stencil gently over frosting. Sprinkle powdered sugar over cupcake; carefully remove stencil.

Makes 12 cupcakes

Tip: Stencils can be found at craft stores and baking supply stores. You can also make your own stencils by cutting out hearts from paper.

Chocolate Lovers' Cupcakes

St. Patrick's Day

Pot of Gold Cookies

4½ cups powdered sugar, divided
1 cup (2 sticks) butter, softened
2 tablespoons packed light brown sugar
¼ teaspoon salt
2 cups all-purpose flour
6 to 8 tablespoons milk
Yellow decorating sugar

1. Beat ½ cup powdered sugar, butter, brown sugar and salt in large bowl with electric mixer at medium speed 2 minutes or until light and fluffy. Add flour, ½ cup at a time, beating well after each addition.

2. Shape dough into 14-inch log. Wrap tightly in plastic wrap; refrigerate 1 hour.

3. Preheat oven to 300°F. Cut log into ½-inch-thick slices; place on ungreased cookie sheets. Use scallop-edged cookie cutter to cut slices to resemble coins, if desired.

4. Bake 20 to 25 minutes or until lightly browned. Cool cookies on cookie sheets 5 minutes; remove to wire racks to cool completely.

5. Place cookies on waxed paper. Combine remaining 4 cups powdered sugar and milk, 1 tablespoon at a time, to make medium-thick pourable glaze. Spread glaze over cookies; sprinkle with yellow sugar. Let stand 30 minutes to allow glaze to set.   *Makes 28 cookies*

Hot Cross Buns

    1 package (¼ ounce) active dry yeast
    1 cup warm milk, divided
2¼ cups all-purpose flour
    1 cup currants
 ½ cup whole wheat flour
 ¼ cup granulated sugar
 ¼ teaspoon salt
 ¼ teaspoon ground nutmeg
    2 eggs, beaten
 ¼ cup (½ stick) butter, melted
 ½ cup powdered sugar
    1 to 2 tablespoons milk or cream

1. Sprinkle yeast over ¼ cup warm milk in small bowl; stir to dissolve yeast. Let stand 10 minutes or until bubbly. Meanwhile, combine all-purpose flour, currants, whole wheat flour, granulated sugar, salt and nutmeg in medium bowl. Blend eggs, butter and remaining ¾ cup warm milk in large bowl.

2. Stir dissolved yeast into egg mixture. Gradually beat in flour mixture until well blended. (Dough will be sticky.) Cover and let rise in warm place 1 hour.

3. Preheat oven to 400°F. Grease 12 standard (2½-inch) muffin cups. Vigorously stir down dough with wooden spoon. Spoon about ¼ cup dough into each muffin cup; smooth tops.

4. Bake 20 minutes or until golden brown. Cool buns in pan 5 minutes; remove to wire rack to cool completely.

5. For icing, blend powdered sugar and milk in small bowl until smooth. Spoon into small resealable food storage bag. Cut off small corner of bag; pipe cross on center of each bun.

Makes 12 buns

Hot Cross Buns

Magically Minty Mini Cupcakes

1 package (about 18 ounces) chocolate cake mix, plus ingredients to prepare mix
2 teaspoons mint extract
1 container (16 ounces) white frosting
Green and white sprinkles, green decorating sugar or Irish-themed candy cake decorations

1. Preheat oven to 350°F. Line 48 mini (1¾-inch) muffin cups with paper baking cups or spray with nonstick cooking spray.

2. Prepare cake mix according to package directions; stir in mint extract. Spoon batter into prepared muffin cups, filling two-thirds full.

3. Bake about 12 minutes or until toothpick inserted into centers comes out clean. Cool cupcakes in pans 2 minutes; remove to wire racks to cool completely. Frost cupcakes; decorate with sprinkles, green sugar or candy decorations. *Makes 48 mini cupcakes*

Super-Lucky Cereal Treats

40 large marshmallows
¼ cup (½ stick) butter
6 cups oat cereal with marshmallow bits
Irish-themed candy cake decorations

1. Line 8-inch square pan with foil, leaving 2-inch overhang on two sides. Generously grease or spray foil with nonstick cooking spray.

2. Heat marshmallows and butter in medium saucepan over medium heat 3 minutes or until melted and smooth, stirring constantly. Remove from heat.

3. Add cereal; stir until completely coated. Spread in prepared pan; press evenly onto bottom of pan with rubber spatula. Let cool 10 minutes.

4. Using foil overhangs as handles, remove bars from pan. Cut into 16 squares. Press candy decorations onto top of treats. *Makes 16 treats*

•St. Patrick's Day•

Magically Minty Mini Cupcakes

White Chocolate Shamrocks

  2 packages (about 16 ounces each) refrigerated sugar cookie dough
½ cup all-purpose flour
    Green food coloring
  1 package (14 ounces) white chocolate candy discs
    Green and white sprinkles

1. Let dough stand at room temperature 15 minutes. Preheat oven to 350°F. Lightly grease cookie sheets.

2. Beat dough, flour and food coloring, a few drops at a time, in large bowl with electric mixer at medium speed until well blended. Reserve half of dough; wrap and refrigerate.

3. Roll out remaining dough to ¼-inch thickness between sheets of parchment paper. Cut out shamrocks using 2-inch shamrock-shaped cookie cutter. Place cutouts 2 inches apart on prepared cookie sheets. Repeat with reserved dough. Refrigerate 15 minutes.

4. Bake 8 to 10 minutes or until set. Cool cookies on cookie sheets 5 minutes; remove to wire racks to cool completely.

5. Microwave candy discs in medium microwavable bowl on HIGH 1 minute. Stir; microwave at additional 15-second intervals until smooth and spreadable. Dip edge of each cookie into melted chocolate; decorate with sprinkles. Let stand on parchment paper 15 minutes or until set.

Makes about 2 dozen cookies

White Chocolate Shamrocks

Celtic Knots

1 package (16 ounces) hot roll mix, plus ingredients to prepare mix
1 egg white
2 teaspoons water
2 tablespoons coarse salt

1. Prepare hot roll mix according to package directions.

2. Preheat oven to 375°F. Lightly grease baking sheets.

3. Divide dough into 16 pieces; shape each piece into 10- to 12-inch rope. Form each rope into interlocking rings as shown in photo; place on prepared baking sheets. Moisten ends of rope at seams; pinch to seal.

4. Beat egg white and water in small bowl until foamy. Brush mixture onto dough; sprinkle with salt.

5. Bake about 15 minutes or until golden brown. Serve warm or at room temperature.

Makes 16 knots

 **Tip** For additional flavor, try different seasonings on the knots instead of salt. Sprinkle them lightly with black pepper or garlic powder and grated Parmesan cheese, poppy seeds or sesame seeds before baking.

Celtic Knots

Mint Chocolate Chip Milk Shakes

2 cups mint chocolate chip ice cream
1 cup milk
2 tablespoons whipped topping
1 tablespoon mini chocolate chips

Combine ice cream and milk in blender; blend until smooth. Pour into two glasses. Top with whipped topping; sprinkle with mini chocolate chips.

Makes 2 servings

Mini Chocolate Pots of Gold

1 package (about 16 ounces) refrigerated sugar cookie dough
¼ cup Dutch-processed unsweetened cocoa powder
1 package (14 ounces) caramels
2 tablespoons milk
2 tablespoons mini yellow candy-coated chocolate pieces
2 tablespoons mini orange candy-coated chocolate pieces
   Yellow decorating sugar

1. Spray 36 mini (1¾-inch) muffin cups with nonstick cooking spray. Beat dough and cocoa in large bowl with electric mixer at medium speed until well blended.

2. Divide dough into 36 equal pieces; roll into balls. Place 1 ball in bottom of each muffin cup. Press dough on bottoms and up sides of muffin cups; refrigerate 15 minutes. Preheat oven to 350°F.

3. Bake 8 to 9 minutes. (Cookies will be puffy.) Remove from oven; gently press down center of each cookie. Bake 1 minute more. Cool cookies in pans 5 minutes; remove to wire racks to cool completely.

4. Heat caramels and milk in small saucepan over low heat, stirring frequently, until melted and smooth. Carefully spoon about 1 tablespoon caramel mixture into each cookie cup. While caramel is still warm, decorate with chocolate pieces and yellow sugar. Cool completely.

Makes 36 treats

·St. Patrick's Day·

Mint Chocolate Chip Milk Shakes

Kelly Green Mini Bundt Cakes

2 tablespoons butter, melted
1 package (about 18 ounces) white cake mix, plus ingredients to prepare mix
   Green food coloring
1 container (16 ounces) white frosting
   Green decorating sugar

1. Preheat oven to 350°F. Brush 12 mini (1-cup) bundt cups with butter.

2. Prepare cake mix according to package directions. Add food coloring to batter, a few drops at a time, until desired shade of green is reached. Fill prepared bundt cups half full.

3. Bake 20 minutes or until toothpick inserted near centers comes out clean. Cool cakes in pans 5 minutes. Carefully place wire racks on top of pans; invert pans. Lightly tap bottom of pans to help release cakes. Cool completely on wire racks.

4. Place frosting in small microwavable bowl. Add food coloring, a few drops at a time, until desired shade of green is reached. Microwave on LOW (30%) 30 seconds or until frosting is pourable but not completely melted. Spoon frosting over cakes. Sprinkle with green sugar.

Makes 12 mini cakes

Variation: Add 1 cup mini semisweet chocolate chips or sprinkles to the batter before adding the food coloring.

Kelly Green Mini Bundt Cakes

Shamrock Cheezies with Herb Dip

½ cup mayonnaise
2 tablespoons chopped fresh herbs (such as parsley, basil or dill)
8 slices American cheese
8 slices sandwich bread
 Butter, melted

1. Combine mayonnaise and herbs in small bowl; mix well. Refrigerate until ready to use.

2. Place 2 cheese slices on each of 4 bread slices; top with remaining bread slices. Brush outsides of sandwiches with butter. Cut sandwiches into shamrocks with shamrock-shaped cookie cutter.

3. Heat large nonstick skillet over medium heat. Add sandwiches; cook 4 to 5 minutes per side or until cheese melts and sandwiches are golden brown. Serve with Herb Dip.

Makes 4 sandwiches

Tip American cheese is always a sandwich favorite with kids, but the type of cheese can be changed to suit different tastes. Try Cheddar, Colby, Meunster, Monterey Jack or Swiss—these and other varieties can be purchased presliced in packages or from the deli counter at the supermarket.

Shamrock Cheezie with Herb Dip

Easter

Easy Easter Cupcakes

    1 package (about 18 ounces) yellow cake mix, plus ingredients to prepare mix
    1 container (16 ounces) white frosting
      Green food coloring
   24 sugar-coated colored marshmallow chicks and/or rabbits
      Round white candies

1. Preheat oven to 350°F. Line 24 standard (2½-inch) muffin cups with paper baking cups.

2. Prepare cake mix and bake according to package directions. Cool cupcakes in pans 10 minutes; remove to wire racks to cool completely.

3. Place frosting in small bowl. Add food coloring, a few drops at a time, until desired shade of green is reached. Frost cupcakes.

4. Trim marshmallow animals with scissors or knife to fit on cupcakes. Place 1 marshmallow on each cupcake. Decorate edges of cupcakes with white candies.   *Makes 24 cupcakes*

Coconut Nests

½ cup sugar
4 egg whites
1½ teaspoons vanilla
¼ teaspoon salt
2 packages (14 ounces each) sweetened flaked coconut
Candy eggs

1. Preheat oven to 350°F. Line two cookie sheets with parchment paper.

2. Whisk sugar, egg whites, vanilla and salt in large bowl until thick and foamy. Add coconut; stir until well blended.

3. Drop coconut mixture by scant ¼ cupfuls 2 inches apart onto prepared cookie sheets. Shape into 2½-inch nests by pressing mixture flat and then pinching up sides.

4. Bake 15 minutes or until bottoms and edges are browned and nests are no longer shiny, rotating cookie sheets halfway through baking time. Cool nests on cookie sheets 10 minutes; remove to wire racks to cool completely. (Nests will stiffen slightly when cool.) Fill nests with candy eggs.   *Makes about 32 nests*

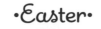

Coconut Nests

Crazy Creature Brownies

1¼ cups granulated sugar
¾ cup (1½ sticks) butter
½ cup unsweetened cocoa powder
2 eggs
1 teaspoon vanilla
½ teaspoon baking soda
½ teaspoon baking powder
1½ cups all-purpose flour
1 cup buttermilk
3 cups powdered sugar, sifted
⅓ cup orange juice, apple juice or milk
Food coloring
Sprinkles, dragées and decors

1. Preheat oven to 350°F. Line 15×10-inch jelly-roll pan with heavy-duty foil, leaving 1-inch overhang over edges. Spray foil with nonstick cooking spray.

2. Combine granulated sugar, butter and cocoa in large saucepan. Cook and stir over low heat until butter is melted and mixture is smooth. Remove from heat; cool 5 minutes.

3. Beat in eggs until well blended. Add vanilla, baking soda and baking powder; mix well. Alternately add flour and buttermilk, stirring after each addition until well blended. Spread batter evenly in prepared pan.

4. Bake 20 to 22 minutes or until center is firm to the touch. Cool completely in pan on wire rack. Use foil to lift brownies out of pan. Cut out animals with 2- to 3-inch animal-shaped cookie cutters. Place brownies on wire rack set over waxed paper.

5. Combine powdered sugar and orange juice in medium bowl until well blended. Tint glaze with food coloring. Spread glaze over brownies; decorate with sprinkles, dragées and decors as desired. Let stand about 20 minutes or until set. *Makes about 2 dozen brownies*

Crazy Creature Brownies

Crispy Kaleidoscope Eggs

    3 tablespoons butter
    3 cups mini marshmallows
  2½ cups crisp rice cereal
    2 cups fruit-flavored ring-shaped cereal
    ½ cup jelly beans

1. Microwave butter in large microwavable bowl on HIGH 1 minute or until completely melted.

2. Add marshmallows, cereals and jelly beans to bowl; microwave on HIGH 1 minute. Stir gently to combine ingredients without crushing cereal. Let stand 2 minutes or until cool enough to handle.

3. Butter hands well. Form ¼ cupfuls of cereal mixture into egg shapes (about the size of real eggs). Mixture will remain moldable for about 10 minutes.

Makes about 2 dozen eggs

 *Tip* Working with a melted marshmallow mixture can be sticky business! Follow the recipe directions to butter your hands well in order to minimize sticking. Or, you can spray your hands with nonstick cooking spray or dampen them with water instead.

Crispy Kaleidoscope Eggs

Citrus Easter Chicks

1 package (about 16 ounces) refrigerated sugar cookie dough
⅓ cup all-purpose flour
1½ teaspoons lemon extract
Lemon Cookie Glaze (recipe follows)
2 cups shredded coconut, tinted yellow*
Mini semisweet chocolate chips, assorted candies and decors

To tint coconut, combine small amount of food coloring (paste or liquid) with 1 teaspoon water in large bowl. Add coconut and stir until evenly coated. Add more food coloring, if needed.

1. Let dough stand at room temperature 15 minutes. Beat dough, flour and lemon extract in large bowl with electric mixer at medium speed until well blended. Divide dough into 2 discs. Wrap and refrigerate 1 hour.

2. Preheat oven to 350°F. Working with one disc at a time, roll out dough to ¼-inch thickness between sheets of parchment paper. Cut out chicks with 2- to 3-inch chick-shaped cookie cutters. Place 2 inches apart on ungreased cookie sheets.

3. Bake 7 to 9 minutes or until set. Cool cookies on cookie sheets 5 minutes; remove to wire racks to cool completely.

4. Place wire racks over parchment paper. Prepare Lemon Cookie Glaze; spread over cookies. Sprinkle with coconut. Decorate chicks with mini chocolate chips, candies and decors as desired. Let stand 40 minutes or until set.   *Makes about 1½ dozen cookies*

Lemon Cookie Glaze: Combine 4 cups powdered sugar, ¼ cup lemon juice and ½ teaspoon lemon peel in medium bowl until well blended. Add additional lemon juice, 1 teaspoon at a time, to make pourable glaze. Stir in yellow food coloring, a few drops at a time, until desired shade of yellow is reached.

Citrus Easter Chicks

Brownie Eggs

¾ cup (1½ sticks) butter
4 squares (1 ounce each) unsweetened chocolate
1¾ cups sugar
4 eggs
1 teaspoon vanilla
1 cup all-purpose flour
½ teaspoon salt
1 cup white chocolate chips
Pink and purple decorating icings
Colored candy dots

1. Preheat oven to 350°F. Spray 13×9-inch baking pan with nonstick cooking spray.

2. Heat butter and chocolate in medium saucepan over very low heat, stirring frequently, until melted and smooth. Remove pan from heat.

3. Gradually stir in sugar until well blended. Add eggs, one at a time, mixing well after each addition. Stir in vanilla. Combine flour and salt in small bowl; stir into chocolate mixture until blended. Stir in chocolate chips. Spread batter evenly in prepared pan.

4. Bake about 23 minutes or until toothpick inserted into center comes out with fudgy crumbs. Cool completely in pan on wire rack.

5. Cut out eggs with 2- to 3-inch egg-shaped cookie cutter; decorate with icings and candies.

Makes about 2 dozen eggs

Brownie Eggs

Easter Nest Cookies

1½ cups all-purpose flour
1 teaspoon baking powder
½ teaspoon salt
¾ cup (1½ sticks) butter
2 cups miniature marshmallows
½ cup sugar
1 egg white
1 teaspoon vanilla extract
½ teaspoon almond extract
3¾ cups MOUNDS® Sweetened Coconut Flakes, divided
    JOLLY RANCHER® Jelly Beans
    HERSHEY'S Candy-Coated Milk Chocolate Eggs

1. Heat oven to 375°F.

2. Stir together flour, baking powder and salt; set aside. Place butter and marshmallows in microwave-safe bowl. Microwave at HIGH (100%) 1 to 1½ minutes or just until mixture melts when stirred. Beat sugar, egg white, vanilla and almond extract in separate bowl; add melted butter mixture, beating until light and fluffy. Gradually add flour mixture, beating until blended. Stir in 2 cups coconut.

3. Shape dough into 1-inch balls; roll balls in remaining 1¾ cups coconut, tinting coconut, if desired.* Place balls on ungreased cookie sheet. Press thumb into center of each ball, creating shallow depression.

4. Bake 8 to 10 minutes or just until lightly browned. Place 1 to 3 jelly beans and milk chocolate eggs in center of each cookie. Transfer to wire rack; cool completely.

Makes about 3½ dozen cookies

To tint coconut: Place ¾ teaspoon water and a few drops food color in small bowl; stir in 1¾ cups coconut. Toss with fork until evenly tinted.

·Easter·

Easter Nest Cookies

Eggs-Cellent Easter Cookies

  1 package (about 16 ounces) refrigerated sugar cookie dough
¼ cup all-purpose flour
  1 cup plus 1 tablespoon powdered sugar, divided
  1 teaspoon almond extract
    Green food coloring
  1 package (3 ounces) cream cheese, softened
  1 tablespoon butter, softened
    Pink or red food coloring
½ cup shredded sweetened coconut
    Colored decorating icings and gels

1. Let dough stand at room temperature 15 minutes. Preheat oven to 350°F. Grease cookie sheets.

2. Beat dough, flour, 1 tablespoon powdered sugar, almond extract and green food coloring in large bowl with electric mixer at medium speed until well blended and evenly colored.

3. Shape dough into 40 (2½-inch-long) egg shapes. Place 2 inches apart on prepared cookie sheets.

4. Bake 8 to 10 minutes or until set and edges are lightly browned. Cool cookies on cookie sheets 2 minutes; remove to wire racks to cool completely.

5. Beat cream cheese, butter, remaining 1 cup powdered sugar and pink food coloring in medium bowl with electric mixer at medium speed until smooth and desired shade of pink is reached. Stir in coconut.

6. Spread pink filling on 20 cookies. Top with remaining 20 cookies to form sandwiches. Decorate tops of sandwiches with colored icings and gels as desired. Let stand until set. Store in refrigerator. *Makes 20 sandwich cookies*

Eggs-Cellent Easter Cookies

4th of July

High-Flying Flags

¾ cup (1½ sticks) butter, softened
¼ cup granulated sugar
¼ cup packed light brown sugar
1 egg yolk
1¾ cups all-purpose flour
¾ teaspoon baking powder
⅛ teaspoon salt
Lollipop sticks
Blue decorating icing, white sugar stars, white decorating icing and red string licorice

1. Beat butter, granulated sugar, brown sugar and egg yolk in large bowl with electric mixer at medium speed until creamy. Add flour, baking powder and salt; beat until well blended. Wrap dough in plastic wrap; refrigerate 1 hour or until firm.

2. Preheat oven to 350°F. Grease cookie sheets. Roll dough to ¼-inch thickness on lightly floured surface. Cut out flags with 3-inch flag-shaped cookie cutter. Place lollipop stick under left side of each flag; press gently to adhere. Place flags 2 inches apart on prepared cookie sheets.

3. Bake 8 to 10 minutes or until edges are lightly browned. Remove cookies to wire racks to cool completely.

4. Spread blue icing in square in upper left corner of each flag; arrange sugar stars on blue icing. Spread white icing over plain sections of cookies. Place strips of licorice on white icing to resemble stripes of flag.

Makes 3 dozen cookies

Rocket Pops

1 package (4-serving size) JELL-O® Brand Cherry Flavor Gelatin
1 cup sugar, divided
2 cups boiling water, divided
    Ice cubes
2 cups cold water
1 package (4-serving size) JELL-O® Brand Berry Blue Flavor Gelatin Dessert
1 tub (8 ounces) COOL WHIP® Whipped Topping, thawed

COMBINE dry cherry gelatin mix and ½ cup of the sugar in medium bowl. Add 1 cup of the boiling water; stir at least 2 minutes until gelatin is completely dissolved. Add enough ice cubes to 1 cup of the cold water to measure 2 cups. Add to gelatin; stir until ice is completely melted. Pour evenly into 16 (5-ounce) paper or plastic cups, adding about ¼ cup of the gelatin to each cup. Freeze 1 hour.

MEANWHILE, combine dry blue gelatin mix and remaining ½ cup sugar in medium bowl. Add remaining 1 cup boiling water; stir at least 2 minutes until gelatin is completely dissolved. Add enough ice cubes to remaining 1 cup cold water to measure 2 cups. Add to gelatin; stir until ice is completely melted. Refrigerate 1 hour.

SPOON about 3 tablespoons of the whipped topping over cherry gelatin in each cup; top evenly with blue gelatin, adding about ¼ cup of the gelatin to each cup. Freeze 1 hour or until almost firm. Insert wooden pop stick or plastic spoon into center of each cup for handle. Freeze an additional 4 hours or overnight. To remove pops from cups, place bottoms of cups under warm running water for 15 seconds. Press firmly on bottoms of cups to release pops. (Do not twist or pull pop stick.) Store leftover pops in freezer. *Makes 16 servings*

Note: Wooden pop sticks can be found at craft stores.

Prep Time: 30 minutes

Total Time: 7 hours 30 minutes (includes freezing)

Rocket Pops

Liberty's Torches

24 flat-bottomed ice cream cones
1 package (about 18 ounces) cake mix, any flavor, plus ingredients to prepare mix
1 container (16 ounces) white frosting
   Yellow food coloring
24 red, yellow and orange fruit roll-ups

1. Preheat oven to 350°F. Stand ice cream cones in 13×9-inch pan or in muffin cups.

2. Prepare cake mix according to package directions; fill each cone with 2½ tablespoons batter. Bake 30 minutes or until toothpick inserted into centers comes out clean. Remove cones to wire racks to cool completely.

3. Place frosting in small bowl. Add food coloring, a few drops at a time, until desired shade of yellow is reached. Pipe or spread frosting on cupcakes.

4. Cut pointy flames from fruit roll-ups using kitchen scissors or sharp knife. Fold or roll flames to stand upright; arrange on cupcakes before frosting sets.   *Makes 24 cupcakes*

Tip If you have a pastry bag, use a writing tip to pipe the frosting and create the yellow flames on these cupcakes. If not, a resealable food storage bag works just as well—simply transfer the frosting to the bag with a spatula, twist the bag at the top just above the frosting, and cut off a small corner of the bag.

Liberty's Torches

Patriotic Cocoa Cupcakes

    2 cups sugar
1¾ cups all-purpose flour
 ¾ cup HERSHEY'S Cocoa
    2 teaspoons baking soda
    1 teaspoon baking powder
    1 teaspoon salt
    2 eggs
    1 cup buttermilk or sour milk*
    1 cup boiling water
 ½ cup vegetable oil
    1 teaspoon vanilla extract
      Vanilla Frosting (recipe follows)
      Chocolate stars or blue and red decorating icings (in tubes)

*To sour milk: Use 1 tablespoon white vinegar plus milk to equal 1 cup.

1. Heat oven to 350°F. Grease and flour muffin cups (2½ inches in diameter) or line with paper bake cups.

2. Combine dry ingredients in large bowl. Add eggs, buttermilk, water, oil and vanilla; beat on medium speed of mixer 2 minutes (batter will be thin). Fill cups ⅔ full with batter.

3. Bake 15 minutes or until wooden pick inserted in centers comes out clean. Remove cupcakes from pan. Cool completely. To make chocolate stars for garnish, if desired, cut several cupcakes into ½-inch slices; cut out star shapes from cake slices. Frost remaining cupcakes. Garnish with chocolate stars or with blue and red decorating icings.

Makes about 30 cupcakes

Vanilla Frosting: Beat ¼ cup (½ stick) softened butter, ¼ cup shortening and 2 teaspoons vanilla extract in large bowl. Add 1 cup powdered sugar; beat until creamy. Add 3 cups powdered sugar alternately with 3 to 4 tablespoons milk, beating to spreading consistency. Makes about 2⅓ cups frosting.

Patriotic Cocoa Cupcakes

Declaration of Independence

  1 package (11 ounces) refrigerated French bread dough
  3 tablespoons butter, melted
  3 tablespoons sugar
  ¾ teaspoon ground cinnamon
    Black decorating gel

1. Preheat oven to 350°F. Spray nonstick baking sheet with nonstick cooking spray.

2. Unroll dough on prepared baking sheet; press into 14×10-inch rectangle. Roll up short ends of dough about 1 inch to resemble scroll.

3. Brush butter over dough. Combine sugar and cinnamon in small bowl; sprinkle over dough.

4. Bake on center oven rack 10 to 11 minutes or just until edges are light golden. Cool completely on wire rack.

5. Use decorating gel to write "Declaration of Independence" and "July 4, 1776" across top of scroll and sign declaration, if desired. *Makes about 8 servings*

Note: Decorating gel comes in small tubes and is easy to use for writing. However, gel does not harden when it dries like icing does, so be careful when handling the finished product.

Declaration of Independence

American Flag Pizzas

  2 packages (about 14 ounces each) refrigerated pizza crust
  2 cups prepared pizza sauce
 1⅓ cups shredded sharp Cheddar cheese
 12 cheese sticks or string cheese (about 1 ounce each), quartered lengthwise
      (48 pieces total)
 25 slices pepperoni, quartered

1. Preheat oven to 400°F. Lightly spray two nonstick 17×11-inch baking sheets with nonstick cooking spray.

2. Unroll pizza crusts on prepared baking sheets. Starting at center, press dough to edges of baking sheets. Bake on center oven rack 8 minutes.

3. Spread 1 cup pizza sauce evenly over each crust. Sprinkle ⅔ cup Cheddar cheese on upper left quarter of each pizza. Arrange 24 cheese strips, end to end, on each pizza to resemble stripes of American flag. Place 50 pepperoni quarters on top of Cheddar cheese to resemble stars.

4. Bake pizzas on center oven rack, one at a time, 8 minutes or until cheese is melted and edges are golden brown. *Do not overbake.* *Makes 16 servings*

American Flag Pizza

Ice Cream Uncle Sams

1½ quarts vanilla ice cream
2 to 3 blue fruit roll-ups
2 to 3 red fruit roll-ups
12 flat-bottomed ice cream cones
1 tube blue decorating icing
1 tube red decorating icing
White star-shaped decors
1 can (16 ounces) vanilla frosting with decorative tips
Candy-coated chocolate pieces

1. Scoop ice cream into 12 (½-cup) scoops on baking sheet. Place in freezer at least 1 hour.

2. Unroll blue fruit roll-ups on work surface. Cut lengthwise into 12 strips (each about 7½ inches long and 1 inch wide) with sharp knife. Unroll red fruit roll-ups on work surface. Cut into 60 strips (each about 2 inches long and ½ inch wide).

3. Stand one ice cream cone upside down. Wrap 1 blue fruit strip around widest part of cone; secure with blue icing. Attach 5 red fruit strips vertically around narrow end of cone with red icing, spacing strips evenly around cone. Attach stars to blue hat band with frosting. Repeat with remaining cones.

4. Place ice cream scoops on serving plate; top each with hat. Working quickly, press chocolate pieces into ice cream to create eyes. Add hair, beards and eyebrows with frosting and star and leaf tips. Pipe noses and mouths with red icing. Freeze until ready to serve.

Makes 12 servings

Ice Cream Uncle Sams

American Berry No-Bake Cheesecake

  2 packages (8 ounces each) PHILADELPHIA® Cream Cheese, softened
⅓ cup sugar
  2 cups thawed COOL WHIP® Whipped Topping
  1 HONEY MAID® Graham Pie Crust (6 ounces)
  1 pint (2 cups) strawberries, halved
⅓ cup blueberries

BEAT cream cheese and sugar in large bowl with electric mixer on medium speed until well blended. Gently stir in whipped topping.

SPOON into crust.

REFRIGERATE 3 hours or until set. Arrange strawberries and blueberries in rows on top of cheesecake to resemble flag. (Or arrange fruit in other desired design on top of cheesecake.) Store leftover cheesecake in refrigerator. *Makes 8 servings*

Tips: Looking for a reduced fat version of this summertime favorite? Save 10 grams of total fat, 6 grams of saturated fat and 90 calories per serving by preparing with PHILADELPHIA® Neufchâtel Cheese, ⅓ Less Fat than Cream Cheese; COOL WHIP LITE® Whipped Topping and a ready-to-use reduced fat graham cracker crumb crust (for a delicious 320 calories and 19 grams of fat per serving).

Best of Season: Omit strawberries and blueberries. Prepare cheesecake as directed. Top with 2⅓ cups combined fresh raspberries and sliced peaches.

Prep Time: 15 minutes (plus refrigerating)

American Berry No-Bake Cheesecake

Halloween

Halloween Hedgehogs

1 package (about 18 ounces) chocolate cake mix, plus ingredients to prepare mix
1 container (16 ounces) chocolate frosting
    White chocolate chips
    Black jelly beans, cut into halves
    Black decorating gel (optional)
3 cups candy corn

1. Preheat oven to 350°F. Line 22 standard (2½-inch) muffin cups with paper baking cups.

2. Prepare cake mix according to package directions. Spoon batter into prepared muffin cups, filling two-thirds full.

3. Bake 18 to 22 minutes or until toothpick inserted into centers comes out clean. Cool cupcakes in pans 10 minutes; remove to wire racks to cool completely.

4. Frost cupcakes. Arrange white chips and jelly bean half on one side of each cupcake to create face; pipe dot of frosting or decorating gel onto each eye. Arrange candy corn around face and all over each cupcake.

Makes 22 cupcakes

Freaky Fondue

4 (10-inch) spinach- or tomato-flavored flour tortillas
1 cup canned cheese dip, Cheddar cheese sauce or salsa con queso
8 almond slices
8 small carrots, peeled
1 small jicama, peeled
1 cup cauliflower florets
1 tablespoon milk
1 tablespoon salsa

1. For tortilla hands, preheat oven to 325°F. Cut tortillas in half. Use small knife to cut each tortilla half into shape of small hand; discard trimmings.

2. Place tortilla cutouts on ungreased baking sheet. To create curved hands, drape cutouts over small bowls or custard cups. Spray both sides of cutouts with nonstick cooking spray. Bake 10 minutes or until lightly browned.

3. For carrot fingers, use small dab of cheese dip to glue almond slice onto narrow end of each carrot to resemble fingernails. For jicama bones, cut jicama into ¼-inch slices; cut rectangle from each slice. Trim ends of rectangles with small knife to resemble bones. Arrange tortilla hands, carrot fingers, jicama bones and cauliflower "brains" on large platter.

4. Stir milk into remaining cheese dip in microwavable serving bowl until blended. Microwave on HIGH 15 seconds or until heated through. Swirl salsa on top. Place warm dip in center of platter; serve immediately. *Makes 8 to 10 servings*

Freaky Fondue

Great Pumpkin Cake

    1 package (2-layer) cake mix, any flavor
    1 package (8 ounces) PHILADELPHIA® Cream Cheese, softened
    ¼ cup (½ stick) butter, softened
    4 cups powdered sugar
      Few drops each green, red and yellow food coloring
    1 COMET® Ice Cream Cone

PREPARE cake batter and bake in 12-cup fluted tube pan as directed on package. Cool in pan 10 minutes. Invert cake onto wire rack; remove pan. Cool cake completely.

MEANWHILE, beat cream cheese and butter in medium bowl with electric mixer on medium speed until blended. Gradually add sugar, beating until well blended after each addition. Remove ½ cup of the frosting; place in small bowl. Add green food coloring; stir until well blended. Spread half of the green frosting onto outside of ice cream cone; set aside. Cover and reserve remaining green frosting for later use.

ADD red and yellow food colorings to remaining white frosting to tint it orange. Spread onto cake to resemble pumpkin. Invert ice cream cone in hole in top of cake for pumpkin's stem. Pipe reserved green frosting in vertical lines down side of cake.

Makes 24 servings (1 slice each)

Cooking Know-How: For a more rounded Great Pumpkin Cake, use a tall 12-cup fluted tube pan. As the cake bakes, it rises and forms a rounded top. When the cake is unmolded (upside-down), the bottom of the cake will be rounded. If the cake is baked in a shorter 12-cup fluted tube pan, the resulting cake will be flatter.

Fun Idea: Place black gumdrops on sheet of waxed paper sprinkled with granulated sugar. Use a rolling pin to flatten each gumdrop, turning frequently to coat both sides with sugar. Cut into desired shapes with a sharp knife. Use to decorate a frosted cake to resemble a jack-o'-lantern.

Great Pumpkin Cake

Sinister Slushies

4 bottles brightly colored sports drinks
4 to 8 ice cube trays

1. Pour each sports drink into separate ice cube trays; freeze overnight.

2. Just before serving, place each color ice cubes in separate large resealable food storage bags. Seal bags; crush cubes with rolling pin.

3. Layer different colors of ice slush in clear glasses. Serve with straws, if desired.

Makes 4 to 8 servings

Monster Finger Sandwiches

1 package (11 ounces) refrigerated breadstick dough (12 breadsticks)
  Mustard
12 slices deli ham, cut into ½-inch strips
4 slices Monterey Jack cheese, cut into ½-inch strips
1 egg yolk
  Food coloring

1. Preheat oven to 350°F. Place 6 breadsticks on ungreased baking sheet; spread with mustard. Divide ham strips evenly among breadsticks; place on mustard. Place cheese strips over ham. Top with remaining 6 breadsticks. Gently stretch top breadsticks over filling; press top and bottom breadsticks together to seal.

2. Use sharp knife to score knuckle and nail lines into each sandwich. (Do not cut completely through dough.) Place egg yolk in small bowl; add food coloring, a few drops at a time, until desired shade is reached. Paint nails with egg yolk mixture.

3. Bake on lower oven rack 12 to 13 minutes or just until light golden. Let cool slightly. Serve warm or cool completely.

Makes 6 servings

Sinister Slushies

Sugar & Spice Halloween Cookies

2⅓ cups all-purpose flour
  2 teaspoons ground cinnamon
1½ teaspoons baking powder
1½ teaspoons ground ginger
 ½ teaspoon salt
 ¼ teaspoon nutmeg
 ¾ cup (1½ sticks) butter, softened
 ½ cup packed brown sugar
 ½ cup molasses
  1 egg
   Colored frostings and sparkling sugars

1. Combine flour, cinnamon, baking powder, ginger, salt and nutmeg in medium bowl. Beat butter and brown sugar in large bowl with electric mixer at medium speed until light and fluffy. Add molasses and egg; beat until well blended. Gradually beat in flour mixture just until combined.

2. Form dough into 2 balls; press into 2-inch-thick discs. Wrap in plastic wrap; refrigerate at least 1 hour or until firm. (Dough may be prepared up to 2 days before baking.) Let stand at room temperature to soften slightly before rolling out.

3. Preheat oven to 350°F. Roll out dough to ¼-inch thickness on lightly floured surface. Cut out shapes with Halloween cookie cutters. Place cutouts on ungreased cookie sheets.

4. Bake 12 to 14 minutes or until centers of cookies are firm to the touch. Cool cookies on cookie sheets 1 minute; remove to wire racks to cool completely. Frost and decorate as desired.

Makes 2 to 3 dozen cookies

Sugar & Spice Halloween Cookies

Witch's Cauldron Pasta with Breadstick Broomsticks

1 pound rotini or cavatappi pasta
1 package (10 ounces) frozen chopped spinach, thawed and squeezed dry
1 package (3 ounces) cream cheese
½ teaspoon ground nutmeg
1 jar (16 ounces) alfredo pasta sauce
Breadstick Broomsticks (recipe follows)

1. Cook pasta according to package directions; drain.

2. Meanwhile, combine spinach, cream cheese and nutmeg in blender or food processor; blend until smooth. Combine spinach mixture and alfredo sauce in medium saucepan over low heat; cook and stir until heated through.

3. Toss hot cooked pasta with sauce in large serving bowl until evenly coated. Serve with Breadstick Broomsticks.

Makes 6 servings

Breadstick Broomsticks

1 package (11 ounces) refrigerated breadstick dough

1. Preheat oven to 375°F. Unroll dough and divide along perforations. For each broomstick, shape breadstick into 8×1½-inch strip; twist one end for handle. Cut 5 or 6 slits (2 inches long) into opposite end; separate dough at slits. Place about 2 inches apart on ungreased baking sheets.

2. Bake 15 to 18 minutes or until golden brown.

Makes 12 breadsticks

Witch's Cauldron Pasta with Breadstick Broomsticks

Spider Web Pumpkin Cheesecake

18 OREO® Chocolate Sandwich Cookies, finely crushed (about 1½ cups)
2 tablespoons butter or margarine, melted
3 packages (8 ounces each) PHILADELPHIA® Cream Cheese, softened
¾ cup sugar
1 can (15 ounces) pumpkin
1 tablespoon pumpkin pie spice
3 eggs
1 cup BREAKSTONE'S® or KNUDSEN® Sour Cream
1 square BAKER'S® Semi-Sweet Baking Chocolate
1 teaspoon butter or margarine

PREHEAT oven to 350°F if using a silver 9-inch springform pan (or 325°F if using a dark 9-inch nonstick springform pan). Mix cookie crumbs and 2 tablespoons butter; press firmly onto bottom of pan. Set aside.

BEAT cream cheese and sugar in large bowl with electric mixer on medium speed until well blended. Add pumpkin and pumpkin pie spice; mix well. Add eggs, 1 at a time, mixing on low speed after each addition just until blended. Pour over crust.

BAKE 50 to 55 minutes or until center is almost set; cool slightly. Carefully spread sour cream over top of cheesecake. Run knife or metal spatula around rim of pan to loosen cake; cool before removing rim of pan.

PLACE chocolate and 1 teaspoon butter in small microwavable bowl. Microwave on MEDIUM 30 seconds; stir until chocolate is completely melted. Drizzle over cheesecake in spiral pattern. Starting at center of cheesecake, pull a toothpick through lines from center of cheesecake to outside edge of cheesecake to resemble a spider's web. Refrigerate 4 hours or overnight. Store leftover cheesecake in refrigerator.   *Make 16 servings*

Make it Easy: For easy drizzling, pour melted chocolate into a small plastic bag. Snip off a small piece from one of the bottom corners of the bag. Gently squeeze the bag to drizzle chocolate over cheesecake as directed.

Spider Web Pumpkin Cheesecake

Snake Calzone

1 loaf (16 ounces) frozen white bread dough, thawed
2 tablespoons mustard, plus additional for decoration
1 tablespoon sun-dried tomato pesto
1 teaspoon Italian seasoning
5 ounces thinly sliced ham
5 ounces thinly sliced salami
¾ cup (3 ounces) shredded provolone cheese
¾ cup (3 ounces) shredded mozzarella cheese
2 egg yolks
2 teaspoons water
Red and yellow food colorings
Olive slices and bell pepper strip

1. Line baking sheet with parchment paper; spray with nonstick cooking spray. Roll out dough on lightly floured surface into 24×6-inch rectangle. Spread mustard and pesto over dough, leaving 1-inch border. Sprinkle with Italian seasoning.

2. Layer ham and salami over dough; sprinkle with cheeses. Brush edges of dough with water. Starting with long side, tightly roll up dough. Pinch edges to seal. Transfer roll to prepared baking sheet, seam side down; shape into S-shaped snake or coiled snake (leave one end unattached to form head on coil).

3. Combine 1 egg yolk, 1 teaspoon water and red food coloring in small bowl. Combine remaining egg yolk, remaining 1 teaspoon water and yellow food coloring in separate small bowl. Paint stripes, dots and zigzags over dough with pastry brush to create snakeskin pattern.

4. Let dough rise, uncovered, in warm place 30 minutes. (Let rise 40 minutes if using coil shape.) Preheat oven to 375°F. Taper one end of roll to form head and one end to form tail. Score tail end to form rattler, if desired.

5. Bake 25 to 30 minutes. Cool slightly. Attach olive slices for eyes and bell pepper strip for tongue with small amount of mustard. Fill center of each olive slice with mustard. Slice and serve warm.

Makes about 12 servings

·Halloween·

Snake Calzone

Popcorn Ghosts

1 package (10 ounces) large marshmallows
¼ cup (½ stick) butter
6 cups popcorn or puffed rice cereal
1 pound white candy coating or white chocolate, melted
24 mini chocolate chips
Black string licorice, cut into 2-inch lengths

1. Combine marshmallows and butter in large saucepan. Cook and stir over medium heat until mixture is melted and smooth. Stir in popcorn; mix well.

2. Form each ghost with about 1 cup popcorn mixture using dampened hands. Let ghosts cool completely on waxed paper.

3. Place ghosts on wire racks set over waxed paper. Spoon melted candy coating over each ghost to cover completely. Use fork to create folds and drapes in coating. Decorate with mini chocolate chips for eyes and licorice for mouths. *Makes about 12 ghosts*

Deadly Diamonds

1 small package (9 ounces) devil's food cake mix, plus ingredients to prepare mix
1 cup marshmallow creme
¼ cup red currant jelly

1. Prepare and bake cake mix in 9-inch square baking pan according to package directions. Cool cake in pan 15 minutes. Remove cake from pan; cool completely on wire rack.

2. Cut cake into 4 strips. Trim edges; cut each strip diagonally to form 4 diamonds (total of 16 diamonds).

3. Just before serving, spread 1 tablespoon marshmallow creme over each diamond. Place jelly in small microwavable bowl; microwave on LOW (30%) 20 to 30 seconds. Stir until melted. Drizzle about ½ teaspoon jelly over each diamond; swirl into marshmallow surface to create dripping effect. Serve immediately. *Makes 16 servings*

Popcorn Ghosts

Thanksgiving

Pumpkin Chocolate Chip Sandwiches

 1 cup solid-pack pumpkin
 1 package (about 16 ounces) refrigerated chocolate chip cookie dough
 ¾ cup all-purpose flour
 ½ teaspoon pumpkin pie spice*
 ½ cup prepared cream cheese frosting

*You may substitute ¼ teaspoon ground cinnamon, ⅛ teaspoon ground ginger and pinch each ground allspice and ground nutmeg for ½ teaspoon pumpkin pie spice.

1. Line colander with paper towel. Place pumpkin in colander; drain about 20 minutes to remove excess moisture.

2. Let dough stand at room temperature 15 minutes. Preheat oven to 350°F. Grease cookie sheets.

3. Beat dough, pumpkin, flour and pumpkin pie spice in large bowl with electric mixer at medium speed until well blended. Drop dough by rounded teaspoonfuls 2 inches apart onto prepared cookie sheets.

4. Bake 9 to 11 minutes or until set. Cool cookies on cookie sheets 3 minutes; remove to wire racks to cool completely.

5. Spread about 1 teaspoon frosting on flat side of one cookie; top with second cookie. Repeat with remaining frosting and cookies. *Makes about 2 dozen sandwich cookies*

Feathered Friends

1 package (19 to 20 ounces) brownie mix for 13×9-inch pan, plus ingredients
    to prepare mix
Red, orange and yellow gummy fish candies
1½ containers (16 ounces each) chocolate frosting
White decorating icing
Mini semisweet chocolate chips

1. Preheat oven to 350°F. Line 12 standard (2½-inch) muffin cups with paper baking cups.

2. Prepare brownie mix according to package directions for cakelike brownies. Divide batter evenly among prepared muffin cups. (Do not fill cups more than two-thirds full.) Bake about 24 minutes or until toothpick inserted into centers comes out clean. Cool cupcakes in pan 5 minutes; remove to wire rack to cool completely.

3. Use sharp knife to cut gummy fish in half lengthwise, creating two thinner fish. (You will need about 6 fish for each cupcake.) Cut tails off of each fish; reserve tails.

4. Frost cupcakes. Arrange gummy fish halves, cut sides facing you, in two rows on one side of each cupcake, pressing cut ends of fish into cupcake as shown in photo.

5. Place remaining frosting in pastry bag or resealable food storage bag with hole cut in one corner of bag. Pipe about 1½-inch ball of frosting on opposite side of each cupcake to create turkey head. Pipe eyes with decorating icing; place mini chocolate chip in center of each eye. Use reserved gummy fish tails to create beaks. Set cupcakes on gummy fish tails to resemble feet, if desired. *Makes 12 cupcakes*

Feathered Friends

Apple Cranberry Leaves

    1 tablespoon butter
    2 medium Granny Smith apples, peeled and chopped
    6 tablespoons whole berry cranberry sauce
    2 tablespoons granulated sugar
    ¼ teaspoon ground cinnamon
    1 egg
    1 teaspoon water
    1 package (15 ounces) refrigerated pie crusts (2 crusts)
    Sparkling sugar (optional)

1. Melt butter in medium skillet over medium heat. Add apples; cook about 8 minutes or until softened, stirring occasionally. Stir in cranberry sauce, granulated sugar and cinnamon; cook 10 minutes or until apples are tender and mixture is thickened. Set aside to cool.

2. Meanwhile, preheat oven to 375°F. Line large baking sheet with parchment paper. Beat egg and water in small bowl until blended. Unroll pie crusts on work surface. Cut out 10 leaves from each crust with 3- to 4-inch leaf-shaped cookie cutter.

3. Place 10 leaves 1 inch apart on prepared baking sheet. Brush edges of leaves with egg mixture. Spoon about 1 tablespoon apple cranberry filling onto center of each leaf; top with second leaf and press edges to seal. Brush tops of leaves with egg mixture; cut vents in top crust with paring knife to resemble veins of leaf. Sprinkle with sparkling sugar, if desired.

4. Bake 13 to 15 minutes or until lightly browned. Cool on wire rack.   *Makes 10 leaves*

Apple Cranberry Leaves

Gobbler Cookies

1 package (about 16 ounces) refrigerated sugar cookie dough
¼ cup all-purpose flour
2 teaspoons ground cinnamon
  Red, yellow, orange and white decorating icings
  Chocolate sprinkles, mini chocolate chips and red string licorice

1. Let dough stand at room temperature 15 minutes. Preheat oven to 350°F. Lightly grease cookie sheets.

2. Beat dough, flour and cinnamon in large bowl with electric mixer at medium speed until well blended. Shape dough into 12 large (1½-inch) balls, 12 medium (1-inch) balls and 12 small (¾-inch) balls.

3. Flatten large balls into 4-inch rounds on prepared cookie sheets; freeze 10 minutes. Bake 9 to 11 minutes or until lightly browned. Remove to wire racks to cool completely.

4. Flatten medium balls into 2¼-inch rounds on prepared cookie sheets; freeze 10 minutes. Bake 8 to 10 minutes or until lightly browned. Remove to wire racks to cool completely.

5. Flatten small balls into 1-inch rounds on prepared cookie sheet; freeze 10 minutes. Bake 6 to 8 minutes or until lightly browned. Remove to wire rack to cool completely.

6. Decorate large cookies with red, yellow and orange icings and chocolate sprinkles to resemble feathers. Arrange medium cookies on large cookies, towards bottom; place small cookies directly above medium cookies. Decorate turkeys with icings, mini chocolate chips and licorice to create eyes, beaks, gobblers and feet. Let stand 20 minutes or until set.

Makes 1 dozen large cookies

Gobbler Cookies

Holiday Pumpkin Bars

     2 cups all-purpose flour
     2 teaspoons pumpkin pie spice
     1 teaspoon baking powder
 ½ teaspoon salt
 ¼ teaspoon baking soda
 ¾ cup (1½ sticks) butter, softened
     1 cup plus 2 tablespoons packed brown sugar
     1 egg
 1½ cups solid-pack pumpkin
     1 teaspoon vanilla
     1 cup semisweet chocolate chips, melted

1. Preheat oven to 350°F. Spray 13×9-inch baking pan with nonstick cooking spray. Whisk flour, pumpkin pie spice, baking powder, salt and baking soda in medium bowl.

2. Beat butter and brown sugar in large bowl with electric mixer at medium speed about 3 minutes or until very well blended. Beat in egg until blended. Beat in pumpkin and vanilla. (Mixture may look curdled.)

3. Gradually add flour mixture, beating at low speed just until blended. Spread batter evenly in prepared pan.

4. Bake about 25 minutes or until toothpick inserted into center comes out clean. Cool completely in pan on wire rack.

5. Cut out pumpkin and leaf shapes with 2- to 3-inch cookie cutters. Place melted chocolate in pastry bag or small food storage bag with small corner cut off. Pipe veins on leaves and lines on pumpkins with chocolate.

Makes about 1½ dozen bars

Holiday Pumpkin Bars

Pilgrim Hats

Yellow decorating icing
10 chocolate-covered cookies
10 mini peanut butter cups
Red and orange chewy fruit candies

1. Squeeze small amount of icing onto center of each cookie. Place peanut butter cup upside down on top of icing, pressing gently to adhere.

2. Pipe hatband and buckle around base of each peanut butter cup with icing.

3. Press candies with palm of hand to flatten. (Or stretch candies with fingers.) Cut out squares with scissors. Press 1 candy square into center of each buckle.   *Makes 10 hats*

Tip These treats are the perfect holiday project for kids to help out with. It does require a steady hand to pipe the icing, but little kids can unwrap the peanut butter cups and count out the cookies, while bigger kids can press and cut out the fruit candies to decorate the hats.

Pilgrim Hats

Cornucopia Crunchers

½ cup packed dark brown sugar
5 tablespoons butter
1 egg
¼ cup all-purpose flour
½ teaspoon vanilla
Dash salt
⅓ cup finely chopped dry roasted macadamia nuts
Candy corn, mixed nuts or other Halloween candies

1. Preheat oven to 375°F. Grease cookie sheets or line with parchment paper.

2. Beat brown sugar and butter in medium bowl with electric mixer at medium-high speed until light and fluffy. Add egg, flour, vanilla and salt; beat until blended. Stir in macadamia nuts.

3. Drop batter by rounded tablespoonfuls onto prepared cookie sheets, 6 cookies per sheet. Flatten batter into 2-inch discs. (Cookies will spread to about 6 inches.)

4. Bake, one sheet at a time, 6 to 9 minutes or until caramel-colored and firm. *Do not overbake.* Cool cookies on cookie sheet 1 minute. Working quickly with spatula, ease one cookie at a time from cookie sheet. Form into cornucopia shape by hand or by partially wrapping cookie around handle of wooden spoon. Place cornucopias, seam side down, on plate to harden. Return cookies to oven for about 30 seconds if necessary to make them more pliable.

5. Fill cornucopias with candy corn and mixed nuts. Cornucopias may also be used as place cards; insert name tag into each cookie. *Makes 16 cookies*

Tips: For best results, use insulated light cookie sheets and thoroughly cool the cookie sheets between batches.

Cornucopia Crunchers

Autumn Leaves

1½ cups (3 sticks) butter, softened
¾ cup packed light brown sugar
½ teaspoon vanilla
3½ cups all-purpose flour
1 teaspoon ground cinnamon
½ teaspoon salt
⅛ teaspoon ground ginger
⅛ teaspoon ground cloves
2 tablespoons unsweetened cocoa powder
Yellow, orange and red food coloring
⅓ cup semisweet chocolate chips

1. Beat butter, brown sugar and vanilla in large bowl with electric mixer at medium speed until light and fluffy. Add flour, cinnamon, salt, ginger and cloves; beat at low speed until well blended.

2. Divide dough into 5 equal pieces. Stir cocoa into 1 piece until well blended. (If dough is too dry and will not hold together, add 1 teaspoon water; beat until well blended and dough forms a ball.) Stir yellow food coloring into 1 piece until well blended and desired shade is reached. Repeat with 2 pieces and orange and red food coloring. Leave remaining 1 piece plain.

3. Preheat oven to 350°F. Lightly grease cookie sheets. Working with half of each dough color, press colors together lightly. Roll dough to ¼-inch thickness on lightly floured surface. Cut out leaves with leaf-shaped cookie cutters of various shapes and sizes. Place similarly sized cutouts 2 inches apart on prepared cookie sheets. Repeat with remaining dough and scraps.

4. Bake 10 to 15 minutes or until edges are lightly browned. Remove cookies to wire racks to cool completely.

5. Place chocolate chips in small resealable food storage bag; seal bag. Microwave on HIGH 30 seconds; knead bag lightly. Microwave on HIGH for additional 15-second intervals until chips are completely melted, kneading bag after each interval. Cut off small corner of bag. Pipe chocolate onto cookies in vein patterns. *Makes about 2 dozen cookies*

Autumn Leaves

Peanut Butter Pumpkins

  1 package (about 16 ounces) refrigerated peanut butter cookie dough
½ cup all-purpose flour
  3 cups powdered sugar, sifted
  4 to 5 tablespoons milk
    Orange food coloring
    Orange decorating sugar
    Pretzel sticks
    Green chewy fruit candies

1. Line cookie sheets with parchment paper. Combine dough and flour in medium bowl until well blended. Shape tablespoonfuls of dough into balls; place on prepared cookie sheets. Freeze 20 minutes or until firm.

2. Press side of toothpick (not tip) into dough balls from top to bottom to create grooves in pumpkins. Press toothpick into top of each pumpkin to create hole for stem. Freeze 15 minutes. Preheat oven to 350°F.

3. Bake about 12 minutes or until lightly browned. Immediately press toothpick into tops of pumpkins again to re-open small hole for stem. Cool cookies on cookie sheets 5 minutes; remove to wire racks to cool completely.

4. Place wire racks over sheets of waxed paper. Place powdered sugar in medium bowl; whisk in milk until blended. (Glaze should be thick but pourable.) Stir in food coloring until desired shade of orange is reached.

5. Holding bottoms of cookies, dip tops of cookies into glaze, turning to coat. Let excess glaze drip off before placing cookies, right side up, on wire racks. Sprinkle with decorating sugar. Break pretzel sticks into ½-inch pieces; insert into center holes to resemble stems.

6. Press candies with palm of hand to flatten. (Candies can also be stretched with fingers.) Cut out small (¼-inch) leaf shapes with scissors. Arrange leaves around pretzel stems.

Makes about 26 pumpkins

Peanut Butter Pumpkins

Tom Turkeys

 1 cup (2 sticks) butter, softened
½ cup powdered sugar
 2 tablespoons packed light brown sugar
¼ teaspoon salt
 1 egg
 2 cups all-purpose flour
¾ cup chocolate frosting
¼ to ½ cup white frosting
  Red gummy candies
  Mini semisweet chocolate chips
  Red candy-coated sunflower seeds
  Black string licorice
  Red, orange and yellow candy-coated chocolate pieces

1. Beat butter, powdered sugar, brown sugar and salt in large bowl with electric mixer at medium speed 2 minutes or until light and fluffy. Add egg; beat until well blended.

2. Add flour, ½ cup at a time, beating well after each addition. Shape dough into disc; wrap tightly in plastic wrap. Refrigerate at least 1 hour or until firm.

3. Preheat oven to 300°F. Roll out dough to ⅛-inch thickness between sheets of plastic wrap. Cut out turkeys with 2½- to 3-inch turkey-shaped cookie cutter. Place cutouts 1 inch apart on ungreased cookie sheets.

4. Bake 20 to 25 minutes or until edges are light golden brown. Cool cookies on cookie sheets 1 minute; remove to wire racks to cool completely.

5. Combine chocolate frosting and ¼ cup white frosting in medium bowl until well blended; add additional white frosting if lighter color is desired. Frost cookies with thin layer of frosting.

6. Press red gummy candies with palm of hand to flatten; cut out small triangles for beaks. Arrange mini chocolate chips, candy-coated sunflower seeds and red candy triangles on cookies to create turkey faces. Cut ¼-inch lengths from licorice; place on turkey feet. Decorate body of turkeys with candy-coated chocolate pieces.   *Makes about 12 cookies*

Tom Turkeys

Christmas

Holiday Poke Cake

2 baked 9-inch round white cake layers, cooled
2 cups boiling water, divided
1 package (4-serving size) JELL-O® Brand Gelatin, any red flavor
1 package (4-serving size) JELL-O® Brand Lime Flavor Gelatin
1 tub (8 ounces) COOL WHIP® Whipped Topping, thawed

PLACE cake layers, top sides up, in two clean 9-inch round cake pans. Pierce cake with large fork at ½-inch intervals.

STIR 1 cup of the boiling water into each flavor of dry gelatin mix in separate bowls at least 2 minutes until completely dissolved. Carefully pour red gelatin over one cake layer and lime gelatin over second cake layer. Refrigerate 3 hours.

DIP 1 cake pan in warm water 10 seconds; unmold onto serving plate. Spread with about 1 cup of the whipped topping. Unmold second cake layer; carefully place on first cake layer. Frost top and side of cake with remaining whipped topping.

REFRIGERATE 1 hour or until ready to serve. Decorate with fresh raspberries, if desired. Store leftover cake in refrigerator.   *Makes 16 servings*

Variation: To make this recipe for any holiday, just substitute the appropriate flavor JELL-O® Brand Gelatin.

Special Extra: For an easy, festive touch, sprinkle top of cake with holiday-colored sprinkles just before serving.

Christmas Cookie Tree

2 packages (about 16 ounces each) refrigerated sugar cookie dough
2 to 3 tubes (about 4 ounces each) green decorating icing with tips
1 tube (about 4 ounces) yellow decorating icing
1 tube (about 4 ounces) red decorating icing

1. Let dough stand at room temperature 15 minutes. Preheat oven to 350°F. Line two cookie sheets with parchment paper.

2. Roll out one package dough to ¼-inch thickness between sheets of parchment paper. Cut out 7-inch circle* and 6½-inch circle using sharp knife. Transfer circles to prepared cookie sheet. Reserve scraps; wrap and refrigerate.

3. Repeat step 2 with remaining package dough, cutting out 6-inch circle and 5½-inch circle. Transfer to prepared cookie sheet. Bake 10 to 14 minutes or until edges are lightly browned. Cool cookies on cookie sheets 2 minutes. Remove parchment paper to wire racks; cool completely before removing cookies from parchment paper.

4. Repeat step 3, using scraps to make 8 more circles, each ½ inch smaller in diameter. Reduce baking time as circles get smaller.

5. To assemble tree, secure largest cookie to serving platter with icing. Using leaf tip and green icing, pipe leaves around outer edge of cookie. Place small amount of icing in center of cookie. Add next largest cookie and repeat layers, adding cookies from largest to smallest.

6. Pipe garlands around tree with yellow icing. Pipe ornaments with red icing. Serve cookies individually by separating layers or cutting into pieces with serrated knife.

Makes 12 to 15 servings

*Use a compass to draw 12 circles, each one ½ inch smaller, on parchment paper; cut out and use as patterns to cut dough circles. For a free-form look, use various bowls, glasses and biscuit cutters to trace and cut out 12 graduated circles.

·Christmas·

Christmas Cookie Tree

Marty the "Mousse"

2 packages (8 squares each) BAKER'S® Semi-Sweet Chocolate, divided
1 package (8 ounces) PHILADELPHIA® Cream Cheese, softened
½ cup PLANTERS® Walnut Halves
    Decorations: red candy-coated chocolate pieces and small candies

MELT 8 chocolate squares. Beat cream cheese with electric mixer until creamy. Blend in melted chocolate. Refrigerate 1 hour or until firm.

SHAPE into 18 balls using 4 teaspoons chocolate mixture for each; place in single layer on waxed paper-covered baking sheet.

MELT remaining chocolate squares. Dip balls in chocolate, 1 at a time, turning to evenly coat each ball. Return to baking sheet.

PRESS 2 nuts into top of each ball for the moose's antlers. Add decorations for the nose and eyes. Refrigerate until chocolate is firm.   *Makes 18 servings*

Special Extra: Add 1 to 2 teaspoons of your favorite extract, such as peppermint, rum or almond, to chocolate mixture before shaping into balls.

Prep Time: 20 minutes (plus refrigerating)

 *Tip* To soften cream cheese, place the completely unwrapped package of cream cheese in a microwavable bowl. Microwave on HIGH for 15 seconds or until slightly softened.

Marty the "Mousse"

Sweet Snowmen

1 package (about 18 ounces) vanilla cake mix, plus ingredients to prepare mix
1 container (16 ounces) white frosting
22 large marshmallows
1 package (7 ounces) flaked coconut
44 large black gumdrops
Mini orange candy-coated chocolate pieces
Mini chocolate chips
Round green gummy candies
Red pull-apart licorice twists

1. Preheat oven to 350°F. Line 22 standard (2½-inch) muffin cups with paper baking cups.

2. Prepare cake mix according to package directions. Spoon batter into prepared muffin cups, filling two-thirds full. Bake 18 to 22 minutes or until toothpick inserted into centers comes out clean. Cool cupcakes in pans 10 minutes; remove to wire racks to cool completely.

3. Frost cupcakes. Place 1 marshmallow on each cupcake for head, arranging slightly off center. Lightly press coconut into frosting around marshmallow.

4. For each hat, press 1 gumdrop on countertop or between hands to flatten into 2-inch circle. Attach second gumdrop, flat side down, to center of flattened gumdrop with small dab of frosting.

5. Cut chocolate pieces in half with sharp knife. Decorate snowmen with mini chocolate chips for eyes, chocolate pieces for noses and gummy candies for buttons, attaching with frosting. Separate licorice twists into 2-string pieces; cut into 6- to 8-inch lengths and tie around bottom of marshmallows to create scarves. Attach hats to tops of marshmallows with frosting.

Makes 22 cupcakes

Sweet Snowmen

Chocolate Gingerbread Cookies

2¼ cups all-purpose flour
  3 tablespoons unsweetened cocoa powder
2½ teaspoons ground ginger
  ½ teaspoon baking soda
  ½ teaspoon ground cinnamon
  ⅛ teaspoon salt
  ⅛ teaspoon finely ground black pepper
  ½ cup (1 stick) butter, softened
  ½ cup packed light brown sugar
  ¼ cup granulated sugar
  1 tablespoon shortening
  4 squares (1 ounce each) semisweet chocolate, melted and cooled
  2 tablespoons molasses
  1 egg
    White decorating icing (optional)

1. Combine flour, cocoa, ginger, baking soda, cinnamon, salt and pepper in medium bowl. Beat butter, brown sugar, granulated sugar and shortening in large bowl with electric mixer at medium speed until creamy. Add chocolate; beat until blended. Add molasses and egg; beat until well blended.

2. Gradually add flour mixture, beating until well blended. Divide dough in half. Shape each half into disc; wrap each disc tightly in plastic wrap. Refrigerate at least 1 hour.

3. Preheat oven to 350°F. Roll out one disc of dough to ¼-inch thickness between sheets of plastic wrap. Cut out shapes with 5-inch cookie cutters; place cutouts on ungreased cookie sheets. Refrigerate at least 15 minutes. Repeat with remaining dough.

4. Bake 8 to 10 minutes or until cookies are set. Cool cookies on cookie sheets 5 minutes; remove to wire racks to cool completely. Decorate with icing, if desired.

Makes about 2 dozen cookies

Chewy Chocolate Gingerbread Drops: Decrease flour to 1¾ cups. Shape 1½ teaspoonfuls of dough into balls. Place on ungreased cookie sheets; flatten balls slightly. Do not refrigerate before baking. Bake as directed. Makes about 4½ dozen cookies.

·Christmas·

Chocolate Gingerbread Cookies

Snowman Cups

    1 quart (4 cups) cold milk
    2 packages (4-serving size each) JELL-O® Chocolate Flavor Instant Pudding & Pie Filling
   20 OREO® Chocolate Sandwich Cookies, crushed, divided
   10 glass, paper or plastic cups (6 to 7 ounces)
    2 cups thawed COOL WHIP® Whipped Topping
      Assorted decorating gels

POUR milk into large bowl. Add dry pudding mixes. Beat with wire whisk 2 minutes or until well blended. Let stand 5 minutes. Gently stir in 1 cup of the crushed cookies.

SPOON remaining crushed cookies into bottoms of glasses or cups, adding about 2 teaspoons crumbs to each cup; cover with pudding mixture.

DROP spoonfuls of the whipped topping onto desserts to resemble snowmen. Decorate with gels for the "eyes," "noses," "scarves" and "hats." Refrigerate until ready to serve. Store leftover desserts in refrigerator.   *Makes 10 servings (½ cup each)*

Make it Easy: Instead of dropping spoonfuls of the whipped topping onto desserts, fill a resealable plastic bag with whipped topping; seal bag. Using scissors, diagonally snip off one corner from bottom of bag. Squeeze whipped topping from bag to create snowmen. Decorate as directed.

Prep Time: 15 minutes

·Christmas·

Snowman Cups

Santa's Cookie Pizza

¾ cup (1½ sticks) butter, softened
¾ cup sugar
3 egg yolks
1 teaspoon vanilla
1½ cups all-purpose flour
¼ cup unsweetened cocoa powder
¼ teaspoon salt
1 package (12 ounces) white chocolate chips
½ cup plus 1 tablespoon sweetened condensed milk, divided
1 cup mini pretzel twists
1 cup red and green gumdrops
½ cup chopped peanuts
½ cup red and green candy-coated chocolate pieces

1. Preheat oven to 350°F. Lightly spray 12-inch round pizza pan with nonstick cooking spray.

2. Beat butter and sugar in large bowl with electric mixer at medium speed 1 minute. Beat in egg yolks and vanilla until well blended. Sift flour, cocoa and salt into small bowl. Add to butter mixture; beat just until combined.

3. Press dough into prepared pan, building up edge slightly. Refrigerate at least 15 minutes. Prick holes all over dough with fork. Bake 18 to 20 minutes or until firm. Remove to wire rack to cool slightly.

4. Heat white chips and ½ cup condensed milk in medium saucepan over low heat until chocolate is melted, stirring constantly. Reserve one fourth of chocolate mixture; spread remaining mixture evenly over crust. Immediately sprinkle with pretzels, gumdrops, peanuts and chocolate pieces, pressing down gently to adhere.

5. Combine remaining 1 tablespoon condensed milk and reserved chocolate mixture; stir over low heat until blended. Drizzle over pizza. Cool completely on wire rack before cutting into wedges. Store in airtight container. *Makes 16 wedges*

•Christmas•

Santa's Cookie Pizza

Jingle Bells Ice Cream Sandwiches

 1 package (about 18 ounces) devil's food cake mix
 5 tablespoons butter, melted
 3 eggs
 50 hard peppermint candies, unwrapped
 1 quart vanilla ice cream

1. Preheat oven to 350°F. Spray cookie sheets lightly with nonstick cooking spray.

2. Beat cake mix, butter and eggs in large bowl with electric mixer at medium speed 1 to 2 minutes or until blended and smooth. Drop dough by rounded tablespoonfuls 2 inches apart onto prepared cookie sheets.

3. Bake 12 minutes or until edges are set and centers are no longer shiny. Cool cookies on cookie sheets 5 minutes; remove to wire racks to cool completely.

4. Place peppermint candies in medium resealable food storage bag. Seal bag; crush candies with rolling pin or back of small skillet. Place crushed candies in small bowl. Line shallow pan with waxed paper.

5. Place scoop of ice cream onto flat side of one cookie. Top with second cookie; roll edge in crushed peppermints. Place on shallow pan. Repeat with remaining ice cream, cookies and peppermints. Cover pan; freeze until ready to serve. *Makes about 1½ dozen sandwiches*

Jingle Bells Ice Cream Sandwiches

Holiday Treasure Cookies

1½ cups graham cracker crumbs
½ cup all-purpose flour
2 teaspoons baking powder
1 (14-ounce) can EAGLE BRAND® Sweetened Condensed Milk (NOT evaporated milk)
½ cup (1 stick) butter or margarine, softened
1⅓ cups flaked coconut
1¾ cups (10 ounces) mini kisses, milk chocolate or semisweet chocolate baking pieces
1 cup red and green holiday baking bits

1. Preheat oven to 375°F. In medium bowl, combine graham cracker crumbs, flour and baking powder; set aside.

2. Beat EAGLE BRAND® and butter until smooth; add reserved crumb mixture, mixing well. Stir in coconut, chocolate pieces and holiday baking bits. Drop by rounded teaspoonfuls onto greased cookie sheets.

3. Bake 7 to 9 minutes or until lightly browned. Cool 1 minute; transfer from cookie sheets to wire racks. Cool completely. Store leftovers tightly covered at room temperature.

Makes about 5½ dozen cookies

Prep Time: 10 minutes
Bake Time: 7 to 9 minutes

Index

Acknowlegments

The publisher would like to thank the companies and organizations listed below for the use of
their recipes and photographs in this publication.

EAGLE BRAND®

The Hershey Company

Kraft Foods Global, Inc.

METRIC CONVERSION CHART

VOLUME MEASUREMENTS (dry)

1/8 teaspoon = 0.5 mL
1/4 teaspoon = 1 mL
1/2 teaspoon = 2 mL
3/4 teaspoon = 4 mL
1 teaspoon = 5 mL
1 tablespoon = 15 mL
2 tablespoons = 30 mL
1/4 cup = 60 mL
1/3 cup = 75 mL
1/2 cup = 125 mL
2/3 cup = 150 mL
3/4 cup = 175 mL
1 cup = 250 mL
2 cups = 1 pint = 500 mL
3 cups = 750 mL
4 cups = 1 quart = 1 L

VOLUME MEASUREMENTS (fluid)

1 fluid ounce (2 tablespoons) = 30 mL
4 fluid ounces (1/2 cup) = 125 mL
8 fluid ounces (1 cup) = 250 mL
12 fluid ounces (1 1/2 cups) = 375 mL
16 fluid ounces (2 cups) = 500 mL

WEIGHTS (mass)

1/2 ounce = 15 g
1 ounce = 30 g
3 ounces = 90 g
4 ounces = 120 g
8 ounces = 225 g
10 ounces = 285 g
12 ounces = 360 g
16 ounces = 1 pound = 450 g

DIMENSIONS

1/16 inch = 2 mm
1/8 inch = 3 mm
1/4 inch = 6 mm
1/2 inch = 1.5 cm
3/4 inch = 2 cm
1 inch = 2.5 cm

OVEN TEMPERATURES

250°F = 120°C
275°F = 140°C
300°F = 150°C
325°F = 160°C
350°F = 180°C
375°F = 190°C
400°F = 200°C
425°F = 220°C
450°F = 230°C

BAKING PAN SIZES

Utensil	Size in Inches/Quarts	Metric Volume	Size in Centimeters
Baking or Cake Pan (square or rectangular)	8×8×2	2 L	20×20×5
	9×9×2	2.5 L	23×23×5
	12×8×2	3 L	30×20×5
	13×9×2	3.5 L	33×23×5
Loaf Pan	8×4×3	1.5 L	20×10×7
	9×5×3	2 L	23×13×7
Round Layer Cake Pan	8×1½	1.2 L	20×4
	9×1½	1.5 L	23×4
Pie Plate	8×1¼	750 mL	20×3
	9×1¼	1 L	23×3
Baking Dish or Casserole	1 quart	1 L	—
	1½ quart	1.5 L	—
	2 quart	2 L	—